Discarded!

Your dearest wish
will come true.

Found in my
fortune cookie →

Lois Ehlert

Notes from a colorful life

beach lane books

new york · london · toronto · sydney · new delhi

P S

book

L P

A

R

C

S

the

the SCRAPS book

DON'T READ THIS BOOK

(unless you love books and art)

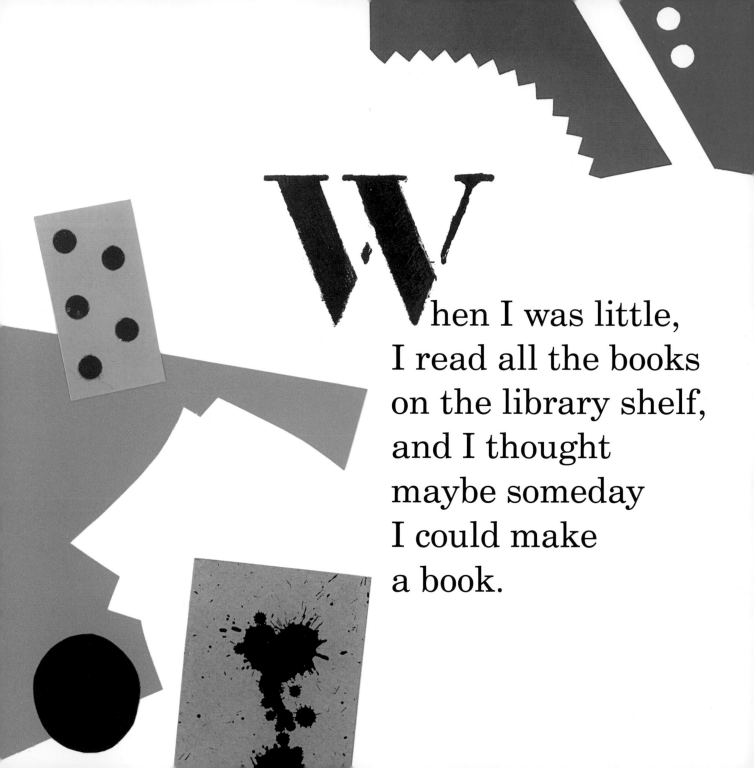

When I was little,
I read all the books
on the library shelf,
and I thought
maybe someday
I could make
a book.

This is me
in my
grandmother's
garden.

My mom and dad returning home after hunting for wild asparagus ↓

photo by my brother, Dick

I was lucky;
I grew up with parents
who made things
with their hands.

Art from
EATING
THE
ALPHABET

This is the home where I grew up.

Mom loved to sew. She had colorful fabric scraps, buttons, lace, ribbons, and many scissors she shared with me.

I use Mom's pinking shears on my → art projects.

Dad had a basement workshop. He gave me wood scraps and taught me how to paint, saw, and pound nails. So I had wonderful art supplies and tools close at hand.

My watercolor brush ↓

Dad's brush ↑

← This is my spot now.

In a small corner
of our house,
Dad set up
a folding table
for me.
It was my spot,
a place to work
and dream.
When I grew up
and left home
for art school,
my table
went with me.

My old folding table →

After art school,
I worked in an
art studio by day

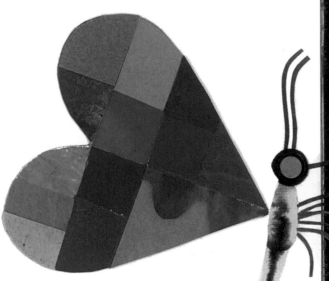

and worked
on book ideas
at night.

I created lots of art, though not for books right away. But I didn't worry. Everyone needs time to develop their dreams. An egg in the nest doesn't become a bird overnight.

Art from HANDS and WAITING FOR WINGS, with added heart wings

This fruit and vegetable face was my first cover idea for EATING THE ALPHABET.

This tomato is on the cover of my first book, GROWING VEGETABLE SOUP.

Where do book ideas come from, anyway? I know I find ideas in the world around me.

I've even found them in my garden or while shopping at the fruit and vegetable store.

Spring Garden Rainbow

In the fall (before frost) plant these bulbs:

- Red Emperor tulips
- Orange Emperor tulips
- Yellow daffodils
- Blue hyacinths
- Purple crocuses
- Green leaves

Plan for bulb garden I planted for my mom

This is the first dummy book for PLANTING A RAINBOW.

and some orange flowers,

tulip

zinnia

tiger

poppy

When a squirrel slipped
into my house, a book idea
walked right up to me!

Scraps of watercolor washes used for NUTS TO YOU!

There he goes —
up the bricks
on his claws.
He steals seeds and
eats with his paws.

American Goldfinch

Art from NUTS TO YOU!

JUMPING

BEAUTIFUL

SMILING

WET

WIGGLY

FANTAILED

SKINNY

DARTING

SCALY

FINNY

SPLASHY

FLIPPING

GLIDING

SHORT

SLENDER

FAT

SLINKY

SLEEK

SLIPPERY

STRIPED

SPOTTED

WIGGLE

SMOOTH

SQUISHY

FLAT

CHUBBY

SLICK

FLUTTER

SWIMMING

FLASHY

GLITTER

On a trip
to the aquarium,
while I watched
colorful fish
swim by,
a book idea swam
into my brain.
I sketched and
made notes
before it floated
away.

Aquarium artis
based on FISH EYES.

You can make a fish aquarium.

Use a discarded snap-top container.

Make paper-fish. Tie with yarn.

Hang fish from top inside container.

I keep my
eyes open.
An idea may
be close by.

Ice fishing decoys
from my collection

JINGLE
JINGLE

Artfrom
FEATHERS
FOR LUNCH

Christmas photo of my sister's cat, Bucky

Once when I visited
my sister, her cat
brushed my ankles
as he escaped
out the door.
A new idea!

First I wrote the story
from the cat's viewpoint.
It went something like this:

Then I wrote the story
from the cat owner's viewpoint.
Here's how it changed:

Door's left open,
just a crack.

Going out,
might not be back!

Food in a can
is not too exciting;

When there are things
I'd rather be biting.

Oh, oh.
Door's left open,
just a crack.

My cat is out,
and he won't come back!

His food in a can
is tame and mild,
so he's gone out
for something wild.

Red-winged Blackbird

carved by my brother →

After writing a story, I sketch the whole book,

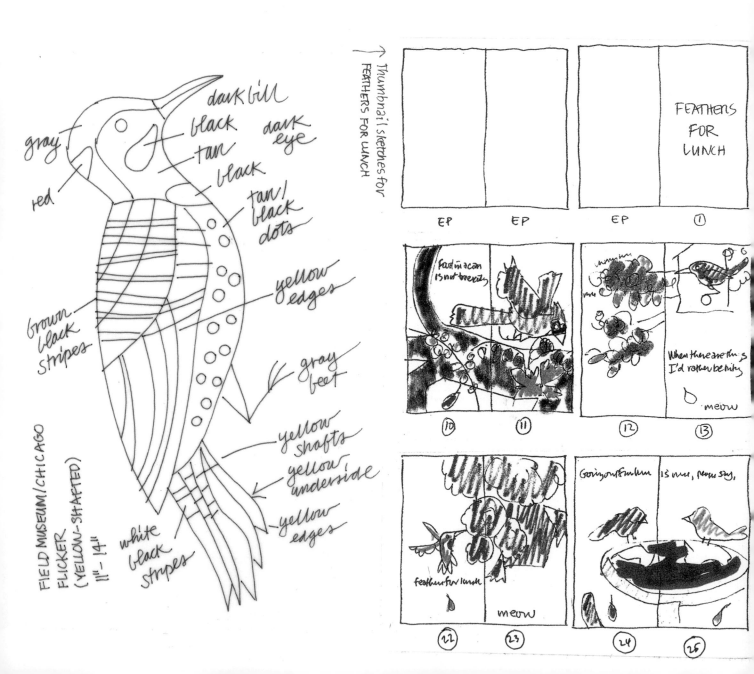

gray

red

dark bill

black

tan

black

dark eye

tan/black dots

yellow edges

brown black stripes

gray feet

yellow shafts

yellow underside

yellow edges

white black stripes

FIELD MUSEUM/CHICAGO
FLICKER
(YELLOW-SHAFTED)
11" - 14"

Thumbnail sketches for
FEATHERS FOR LUNCH

FEATHERS
FOR
LUNCH

EP   EP   EP   ①

food in a can
is not breezy

When there are things
I'd rather be trying

meow

⑩   ⑪   ⑫   ⑬

feathers for lunch

meow

Going out and in
is nice, meow say,

②②   ②③   ②④   ②⑤

figuring out what to illustrate on each page.

Chirping and cheeping, we're sending a warning:

sketch and art from FEATHERS FOR LUNCH

Back and forth, I work on the pictures and words, until together they tell the story.

WHISTLE
WHISTLE
CHECK
CHECK
CHECK

Northern Oriole

lilac bush

Sketch for CHICKA CHICKA BOOM BOOM

My art technique
is called collage.
I cut out scraps,
like pieces of a puzzle,
that I assemble
and glue into place.

Art and color swatches from CHICKA CHICKA BOOM BOOM

RHOD. RED

137

EHLERT

Art from OODLES OF ANIMALS

I'm messy when I work.

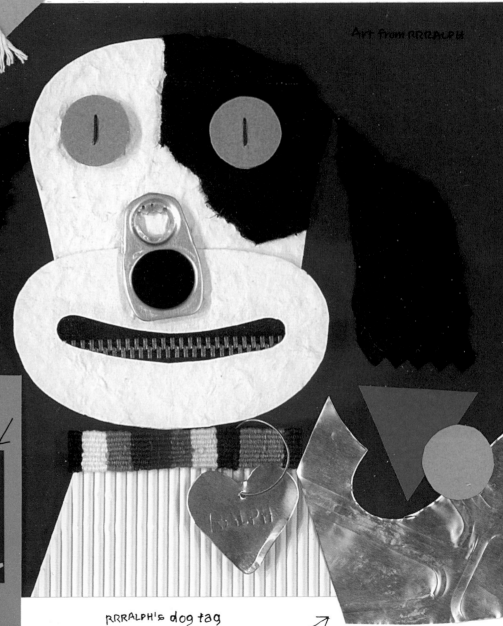

Art from RRRALPH

stencil letter
↓

RRRALPH
typeface
↙

R R

↑
This typeface changed to this.

RRRALPH's dog tag
was cut out of an old pizza pan. ↗

Mechanical sketch
showing die cut overlays
for COLOR ZOO
←

My wastebaskets overflow.

Art from COLOR ZOO

← First idea for COLOR ZOO, created in an artist's bookmaking class, University of Wisconsin

Scraps lie strewn all over the studio, and

more scraps stick to the bottom of my shoes.

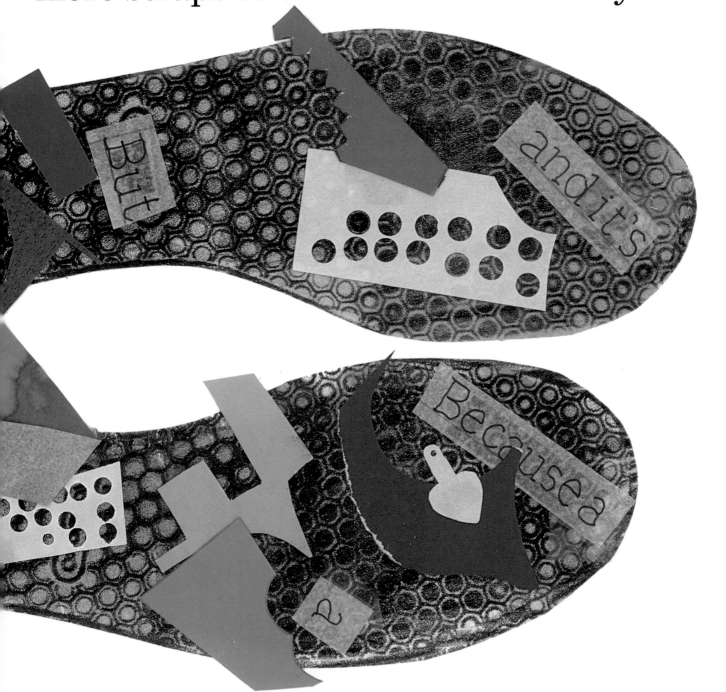

But when ideas are flowing, I keep working.

A Mexican Folktale
Cuckoo
Lois Ehlert

sun/sol
heart/corazón
pepper/pimiento
cuckoo/cucú
dove/paloma
owl/búho

Mexican child's → stick toy

Milagros collected in Mexico ↓

Bird puppet based on
← art from CUCKOO

Bird treat
from
RED LEAF,
YELLOW LEAF

Make a Bird Treat

Use a cookie cutter to cut a heart shape out of a slice of bread. Poke a hole in the top with a pencil or crayon. Brush an egg white onto the bread and press birdseed on top. Let it dry. Then thread a piece of ribbon or yarn through the hole and tie it to a tree.

Now every
night before
I go to bed,
I peek out the
window and
wave to my tree.

bird treat

Downy Woodpecker

suet bag

I often combine real objects with painted ones.

PINE CONE
PEANUT
BUTTER
& SEEDS

LIGHT BLUE
GREY BLUE
BKGD. IS SNOW

WINTER TREE

RIBBONS

I HUNG
FOOD
ON MY TREE
FOR
THE BIRDS
TO EAT.

REAL
NET

bud

bird treat

When it
snows,
I hang up
treats for the birds.

DOWNY
WOODPECKER

Book dummy sketch
for RED LEAF, YELLOW LEAF →

← finished art for the same spread

Art from *Mole's Hill,*
a Woodland Indian folktale

Art from *PIE IN THE SKY*

Art from
LOTS OF SPOTS

↑ Beaded
Woodland
Indian
moccasins

I use odd tools to create texture; I spatter paint with a toothbrush or rub a crayon over my grater.

fiber butterfly,
Peru ↓

Sometimes I photograph folk art from my collection to illustrate a story.

fruit, Mexico

patchwork doll, United States

fruit, Mexico

beaded doll, Africa

doll purse, Bolivia

I use what's close at hand,

sketches for snowballs (made in a hot summer), photo by Lillian Schultz

toy compass

evergreen branch

strawberry

toy wheel

corn

raisin

bottle cap

pencil

cinnamon stick

Mexican scrub brush

seashell

foil candy wrapper

pinecone

toy fish

button

just as I did when I was growing up.

Art from
SNOWBALLS

Guatemalan belt and tie

Sometimes
I go for a walk,
looking for
good stuff.

Crab apples from a tree
near my grocery store
that I used as the cat's
nose in BOO TO YOU!

Black locust seedpods
found in the park that
I used as mouse tails
in BOO TO YOU!

Pumpkin seeds I used
for the cat's teeth in
BOO TO YOU! ⟶

Art from BOO TO YOU!

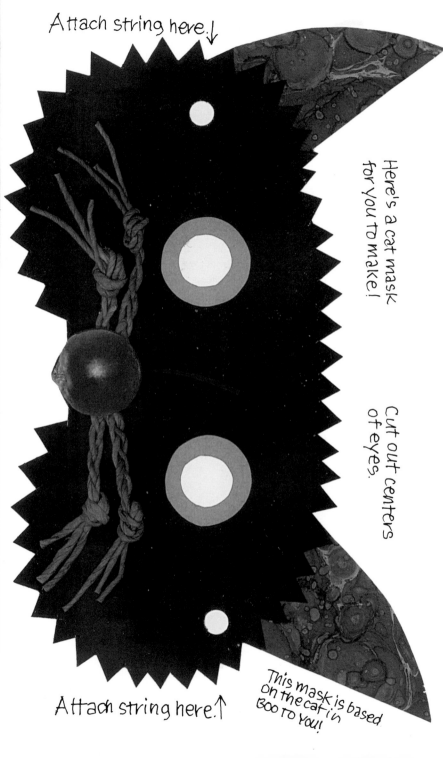

Attach string here.↓

Here's a cat mask for you to make!

Cut out centers of eyes.

This mask is based on the cat in BOO TO YOU!

Attach string here.↑

Mother Nature gives me free art supplies!

Day after day, I work
until the art looks just right to me.

Waiting
for
Wings

Dummy book sketches from WAITING FOR WINGS

They basked
in the sun,
and sipped
as they sat.

THISTLE

PURPLE CONEFLOWER/ECHINACEA
BLACK-EYED SUSAN

MONARCH CATERPILLARS, THE RIDGES, DOOR COUNTY, WI

PHLOX

GAILLARDIA / INDIAN BLANKET FLOWER

You might ask:
why did I choose to be an artist?

Art from
TEN LITTLE
CATERPILLARS

SWEET WILLIAM

Photograph of flowers from a botanical garden, used as reference for art in WAITING FOR WINGS

↑ Make a flower necklace with paper and string.

Art from
WAITING
FOR WINGS

I think maybe it's the other way around. Art chose me.

Photo by my brother, Dick

Art from
TEN LITTLE
CATERPILLARS

This photograph, which I used as reference for the hen in TEN LITTLE CATERPILLARS, was taken years ago at the Wisconsin State Fair. →

If you feel
that way too,
I hope you'll
find a spot to work,
and begin.

Art from
TEN LITTLE CATERPILLARS

I wish you
a colorful life!

Art from
TEN LITTLE
CATERPILLARS

In all things
of nature
there is something
of the
marvelous.

ARISTOTLE

BEACH LANE BOOKS
An imprint of Simon & Schuster Children's Publishing Division
1230 Avenue of the Americas, New York, New York 10020
Copyright © 2014 by Lois Ehlert
BEACH LANE BOOKS is a trademark of Simon & Schuster, Inc.
For information about special discounts for bulk purchases, please contact Simon & Schuster Special
Sales at 1-866-506-1949 or business@simonandschuster.com.
The Simon & Schuster Speakers Bureau can bring authors to your live event.
For more information or to book an event, contact the Simon & Schuster Speakers Bureau
at 1-866-248-3049 or visit our website at www.simonspeakers.com.
Book design by Lois Ehlert and Lauren Rille
The text for this book is set in Century Schoolbook.
Manufactured in China
1213 SCP
First Edition
10 9 8 7 6 5 4 3 2 1
Library of Congress Cataloging-in-Publication Data
Ehlert, Lois.
The scraps book : notes from a colorful life / Lois Ehlert. —1st ed.
p. cm.
ISBN 978-1-4424-3571-1 (hardcover)
ISBN 978-1-4424-3572-8 (eBook)
1. Ehlert, Lois—Juvenile literature. 2. Illustrators—United States—Biography—Juvenile literature.
I. Title.
NC975.5.E36A2 2013
741.6'4092—dc23
2012041869

Art is part of heart.

The moment that I had this box of colors in my hands, I had the feeling that my life was there.
—MATISSE

My thanks to the publishers for granting permission to reproduce
selections from their books.

Houghton Mifflin Harcourt
  Cuckoo, 1997
  Eating the Alphabet, 1989
  Feathers for Lunch, 1990
  Fish Eyes, 1990
  Growing Vegetable Soup, 1987
  Hands, 2004, 1997
  In My World, 2002
  Leaf Man, 2005
  Market Day, 2000
  Mole's Hill, 1994
  Moon Rope, 1992
  Nuts to You!, 1993
  Oodles of Animals, 2008
  Pie in the Sky, 2004
  Planting a Rainbow, 1988
  Red Leaf, Yellow Leaf, 1991
  Snowballs, 1995
  Top Cat, 1998
  Wag a Tail, 2007
  Waiting for Wings, 2001
Richard C. Owen
  Under My Nose, 1996

Simon & Schuster
  Boo to You!, 2009
  Chicka Chicka Boom Boom, 1989,
    written by Bill Martin Jr
    and John Archambault
  Chicka Chicka 1, 2, 3, 2004,
    written by Bill Martin Jr
    and Michael Sampson
  Lots of Spots, 2010
  Mice, 2012, written by Rose Fyleman
  RRRalph, 2011
  Ten Little Caterpillars, 2011,
    written by Bill Martin Jr
HarperCollins
  Angel Hide and Seek, 1998,
    written by Ann Turner
  Circus, 1992
  Color Farm, 1990
  Color Zoo, 1989
  Crocodile Smile, 1994,
    written by Sarah Weeks
  A Pair of Socks, 1996,
    written by Stuart J. Murphy
  Thump, Thump, Rat-a-Tat-Tat, 1989,
    written by Gene Baer

HANDS

growing up to be an artist
Lois Ehlert

Oodles
of
Animals

Lois Ehlert

Growing Vegetable Soup

Lois Ehlert

COLOR FARM

Lois Ehlert

Lois Ehlert

Red,
Leaf,
Yellow
Leaf

Eating
the
Alphabet

Fruits & Vegetables
from A to Z

by Lois Ehlert

Crocodile
Smile

From the creators of CHICKA CHICKA BOOM BOOM

Ten Little Caterpillars

by Bill Martin Jr

illustrated by
Lois Ehlert

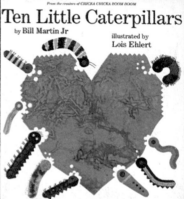

Fish Eyes
A BOOK YOU CAN COUNT ON

Chicka
Chicka
Boom
Boom

Lois Ehlert

by Bill Martin Jr
and John Archambault

illustrated by Lois Ehlert

Chicka
Chicka
1 2·3

Bill Martin Jr
Michael Sampson
Lois Ehlert

Nuts
to
You!

Lois Ehlert

Leaf Man

Lois Ehlert

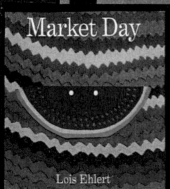

Market Day

Lois Ehlert

Moon Rope

Un lazo
a la
luna

Lois Ehlert

Cuckoo

Cucú   Lois Ehlert

Waiting for Wings   Lois Ehlert

THUMP, THUMP,
Rat-a-Tat-Tat
by Gene Baer
Illustrated by Lois Ehlert

Pie in the Sky
Lois Ehlert

Angel Hide and Seek
by Ann Turner
illustrated by Lois Ehlert

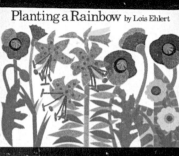
Planting a Rainbow by Lois Ehlert

RRRALPH
Lois Ehlert

Top
Cat
Lois Ehlert

CIRCUS
Lois Ehlert

Feathers for Lunch
Lois Ehlert

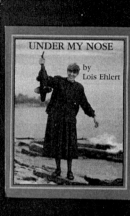
UNDER MY NOSE
by
Lois Ehlert

LOTS
OF
SPOTS
Lois Ehlert

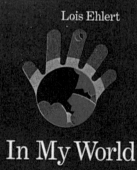
Lois Ehlert
In My World

A
Pair
of
Socks
by Stuart J. Murphy
illustrated by
Lois Ehlert

Snowballs
Lois Ehlert

Mole's
Hill
Lois Ehlert

Boo to You!
Lois Ehlert

WAG A TAIL
Lois Ehlert

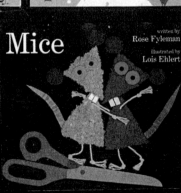
Mice
written by
Rose Fyleman
illustrated by
Lois Ehlert

Dedicated to my editor, Allyn Johnston